The NEHEMIAH CODE

It's Never Too Late *for a* New Beginning

STUDY GUIDE | SIX SESSIONS

O. S. Hawkins

THOMAS NELSON
Since 1798

The Nehemiah Code Study Guide

© 2019 by O.S. Hawkins

Published in Nashville, Tennessee, by Thomas Nelson. Thomas Nelson is a registered trademark of HarperCollins Christian Publishing, Inc.

All Scripture quotations are taken from The New King James Version®. Copyright © 1982 by Thomas Nelson. Used by permission. All rights reserved.

Thomas Nelson titles may be purchased in bulk for educational, business, fundraising, or sales promotional use. For information, please e-mail SpecialMarkets@ ThomasNelson.com.

ISBN 978-0-310-09988-8

First Printing April 2019 / Printed in the United States of America

CONTENTS

INTRODUCTION

*R*ebuilding. Who among us is not in need of an occasional new beginning as we journey through different periods of life? Some of us deal with relationships that need to be rebuilt. Some are in the process of rebuilding businesses. Most coaches are continually engaged in the rebuilding process. Other people are seeking to rebuild their integrity after a misstep. Some are rebuilding their self-confidence. The good news is . . . *it's never too late for a new beginning.*

Nehemiah lived 2,500 years ago, and he "wrote the book" on rebuilding. He was a civil servant—an ordinary guy—who applied some universal principles that enabled him to rebuild a broken city and, in the process, rebuild a lot of broken hopes. His story unfolds many years after the nation of Israel split into two kingdoms. The Northern Kingdom, called "Israel," was ruled by a series of wicked kings until 722 BC, when the Assyrian army swept in and carried the people into a captivity from which they never returned. The Southern Kingdom, called "Judah," lasted until 586 BC, when it was finally devastated and destroyed by the Babylonians.

The Babylonians broke down the walls of Jerusalem, burned its gates, demolished its temple, and led its people away as captives. But after several years, the Persians broke the Babylonian supremacy and allowed some of the Jews to return home. These Jews began to rebuild their temple and city . . . but the sheer magnitude of the task caused them to give up. Years passed. The city, still broken and burned, was in dire need of rebuilding.

In stepped Nehemiah, a Jew still in exile, with a cushy civil service job complete with benefits and retirement. But Jerusalem burned in his heart. So he left Babylon to return to Jerusalem, armed with a focused objective to rally the people, rebuild their hope, and, ultimately, rebuild their holy city. He had a plan for rebuilding, and in the pages of his book, he left us some secrets to his success—a sort of hidden "code," if you will—that can become a fountain of hope and strength to anyone and everyone who will apply his formula.

The journey you are about to make will enable you to apply these marvelous truths so you can rebuild any broken walls in your life and reinforce your own legacy. As you go through this study, I think you will find that Nehemiah's message to you across the centuries is plain and powerful: *It is never too late for a new beginning!*

—O.S. Hawkins

HOW TO USE THIS GUIDE

The Nehemiah Code Video Study is designed to be experienced in a group setting such as a Bible study, Sunday school class, or any small group gathering. Each session begins with a welcome section, several questions to get you thinking about the topic, and a reading from the book of Nehemiah. You will then watch a video with O.S. Hawkins and engage in some small-group discussion. You will close each session with a time of personal reflection and prayer as a group.

Each person in the group should have his or her own copy of this study guide. You are also encouraged to have a copy of *The Nehemiah Code* book, as reading the book alongside the curriculum will provide you with deeper insights and make the journey more meaningful. (See the "For Next Week" section at the end of each between-studies section for the chapters in the book that correspond to material you and your group are discussing.)

To get the most out of your group experience, keep the following points in mind. First, the real growth in this study will happen during your small-group time. This is where you will process the content of the teaching for the week, ask questions, and learn from others as you hear what God is doing in their lives. For this reason, it is important for you to be fully committed to the group and attend each session so you can build trust and rapport with the other members. If you choose to only go through the motions, or if you refrain from participating, there is a lesser chance you will find what you're looking for during this study.

Second, remember the goal of your small group is to serve as a place where people can share, learn about God, and build intimacy and friendship. For this reason, seek to make your group a safe place. This means being honest about your thoughts and feelings and listening carefully to everyone else's opinion. (If you are a group leader, there are additional instructions and resources in the back of the book for leading a productive discussion group.)

Third, resist the temptation to fix a problem someone might be having or to correct his or her theology, as that's not the purpose of your small-group time. Also, keep everything your group shares confidential. This will foster a rewarding sense of community in your group and create a place where people can heal, be challenged, and grow spiritually.

Following your group time, reflect on the material you've covered by engaging in any or all of the between-sessions activities. For each session, you may wish to complete the personal study all in one sitting or spread it out over a few days (for example, working on it a half-hour a day on different days that week). Note that if you are unable to finish (or even start!) your between-sessions personal study, you should still attend the group study video session. You are still wanted and welcome at the group even if you don't have your "homework" done.

Keep in mind the videos, discussion questions, and activities are simply meant to kick-start your imagination so you are not only open to what God wants you to hear but also how to apply it to your life. As you go through this study, be watching for what God is saying to you as learn from Nehemiah's example that *it is never too late for a new beginning.*

Note: If you are a group leader, there are additional resources provided in the back of this guide to help you lead your group members through the study.

GET STARTED RIGHT

Nehemiah 1:1–11

When we are in the process of rebuilding (no matter what it is we are seeking to rebuild), there are not just things that need to be done, but things that need to be undone. There are habits that need to be broken and hearts that need to be healed. Anyone who has ever sought to rebuild a marriage, a business, a dream, or a church knows this to be true. It often is easier to walk away and start over than it is to invest the effort and energy needed for rebuilding. But if we are ever going to be successful in rebuilding, it is essential that we get started right.

O.S. HAWKINS

WELCOME

In 1690, the explorer Alonso De León led an expedition to establish a mission in what was then called Spanish Texas.[1] Several years before, the Spanish authorities had learned the French, their rivals in the region, had established a colony in their territory. De León was dispatched to locate this colony, which he did in 1689.[2] A year later, he returned to build the mission of San Francisco de la Espada. The structure would serve not only as a base of operations for the Spanish but also as a warning to the French not to plant any more colonies in the region.

The builders of the mission knew they had to clear the ground, remove the debris, and build a solid foundation if they wanted the walls of the structure to stand. In other words, they had to *get started right* if they wanted their building project to be a success. But beyond the physical construction, the workers knew they also had to *get started right* with the local people in the region. For the priests at Espada, this meant extending an invitation to the Hasinai, a tribe who had already expressed interest in Christianity, to join in their efforts.[3] In time, the mission would become a place where the local people were not only taught about Christ but also vocational skills such as farming, blacksmithing, weaving, masonry, and carpentry.

In our own rebuilding efforts, we can never underestimate the importance of *getting started right* by having a firm foundation in God's Word. And as we look to the Bible for guidance, we find no greater example of a rebuilder than Nehemiah. Today, we will look at part of his story to see what we can learn about *getting started right* in rebuilding our lives.

SHARE

If you or any of your group members are just getting to know one another, take a few minutes to introduce yourselves. Then, to kick things off, discuss one of the following questions:

- Why is it important for a house to have a strong foundation? What problems will a homeowner have to face if a strong foundation is not in place?

—or—

- What happens when people strike out on a project without first having a good plan in place? When have you been guilty of rushing ahead without a plan?

READ

Invite someone to read aloud the following passage. Listen for fresh insights as you hear the verses being read, and then discuss the questions that follow.

The words of Nehemiah the son of Hachaliah.

It came to pass in the month of Chislev, in the twentieth year, as I was in Shushan the citadel, that Hanani one of my brethren came with men from Judah; and I asked them concerning the Jews who had escaped, who had survived the captivity, and concerning Jerusalem. And they said to me, "The survivors who are left from the captivity in the province are there in great distress and reproach. The wall of Jerusalem is also broken down, and its gates are burned with fire."

So it was, when I heard these words, that I sat down and wept, and mourned for many days; I was fasting and praying before the God of heaven.

And I said: "I pray, LORD God of heaven, O great and awesome God, You who keep Your covenant and mercy with those who love You and observe Your commandments, please let Your ear be attentive and Your eyes open, that You may hear the prayer of Your servant which I pray before You now, day and night, for the children of Israel Your servants, and confess the sins of the children of Israel which we have sinned against You. Both my father's house and I have sinned. We have acted very corruptly against You, and have not kept the commandments, the statutes, nor the ordinances which You commanded Your servant Moses. Remember, I pray, the word that You commanded Your servant Moses, saying, 'If you are unfaithful, I will scatter you among the nations; but if you return to Me, and keep My commandments and do them, though some of you were cast out to the farthest part of the heavens, yet I will gather them from there, and bring them to the place which I have chosen as a dwelling for My name.' Now these are Your servants and Your people, whom You have redeemed by Your great power, and by Your strong hand. O Lord, I pray, please let Your ear be attentive

to the prayer of Your servant, and to the prayer of Your ser-
vants who desire to fear Your name; and let Your servant
prosper this day, I pray, and grant him mercy in the sight of
this man."
   For I was the king's cupbearer (Nehemiah 1:1–11).

1 What is one key insight that stands out to you from this
passage?

2 What steps did Nehemiah take to *get started right* when
faced with a crisis?

WATCH

Play the video segment for session one. As you watch, use the following outline to record any thoughts or concepts that stand out to you.

Notes

Rebuilding is a subject that touches everyone. We all have something that we are "rebuilding" in our lives.

In 586 BC, the Babylonian king Nebuchadnezzar broke down the walls of Jerusalem, burned its gates, and led its people into captivity.

Under the Persians, the Jewish exiles were allowed to return in several waves back to their homeland. But by Nehemiah's day, they still had not rebuilt the city or its walls.

Step 1 in getting started right is to *make an honest evaluation of the situation*. Nehemiah demonstrated this by . . .

Step 2 in getting started right is to *identify with the need.* Nehemiah demonstrated this by . . .

Step 3 in getting started right is to *take personal responsibility.*

- Nehemiah took *personal responsibility* for his people's sin by . . .

- Nehemiah walked in the *fear of God* by . . .

Step 4 in getting started right is to *move out of your comfort zone.* Nehemiah demonstrated this by . . .

DISCUSS

Take a few minutes with your group members to discuss what you just watched and explore these concepts in Scripture.

1 Who are some of the people you know who have needed to go through a time of rebuilding? What are some times you had to go through your own rebuilding process?

2 In what ways did Nehemiah make an honest evaluation of the situation? Why is this such an important first step in any rebuilding effort?

3 How do we know that Nehemiah identified with the need of his people? Why is this step especially important in rebuilding any broken relationships in our lives?

4 Why did Nehemiah feel the need to take personal responsibility for his people's sin? What would have happened if he blamed others for the state of affairs in Jerusalem?

5 Nehemiah was informed that the remnant in Jerusalem had become a "reproach" or a "disgrace" to God. Why did this serve as a strong motivation for him to act?

6 How do we know that Nehemiah moved out of his comfort zone? When are some times that God has called you to take a risk for Him? What was the result?

RESPOND

Briefly review the outline for the video teaching and any notes you took. In the space below, write down the most significant point you took away from this session.

PRAY

End the gathering by partnering with one or two people from your group and praying for each another. Pray especially that God would help you to get started right in your own rebuilding efforts by making an honest evaluation of your situation, identifying with the need, taking personal responsibility, and moving out of your comfort zones. Write down any specific requests in the space below so you can remember to continue praying throughout the week.

BETWEEN-SESSIONS PERSONAL STUDY

*R*ebuilders get started right . . . and when they do, they discover it is never too late for a new beginning. This week, start your rebuilding process right by spending some time with God each day. Reflect on the material you covered during your group time by engaging in any or all of the following between-sessions activities. Be sure to read the reflection questions after each activity and make a few notes in your guide about the experience. At the start of the next session you will have a few minutes to share any insights you learned . . . but remember, the primary goal of these questions is for your own spiritual growth and private reflection.

STARTING BLOCKS

When Nehemiah heard the report that the walls of Jerusalem were broken and the gates were burned, it caused him great sadness. So much sadness, in fact, that when the king asked what was troubling him, Nehemiah requested permission to return to Jerusalem to rebuild the wall. The king granted Nehemiah's request, and he made preparations for the journey home.

In many ways, the news about Jerusalem served as a "starting block" that got Nehemiah motivated for action. In running events, sprinters use starting blocks to hold their feet in place at the beginning of the race. The blocks give the runner an advantage, as he or she can push off them to gain momentum when the starting gun sounds. With this in mind, take a few minutes to reflect on the "starting blocks" in your own life as you respond to the following questions.

1 Have you ever watched a friend, family member, colleague, or teammate struggle to get out of a starting block in a particular situation? What was the situation? Why do you think it was so hard for them to get started?

2 What encouragement or advice did you give to that person in the moment? Or what kind of advice would you have given if he or she had asked you?

3 Think back to when you were a child. What were some of the hardest starting blocks in your childhood (*learning to tie your shoes, riding your bike, starting school*)?

4 What made a difference for you in those starting blocks? How did the support of others and the examples you witnessed help to guide you?

5 Now consider the starting blocks in your adult life. Where have you had the most trouble getting started on something big in your life (*a project, a new business, getting more involved in your community*)?

6 Why do you think it is so hard to get started? What are some thoughts or excuses that have kept you from getting out of the starting blocks?

7 How did it feel to actually get started? What was your experience like?

8 Nehemiah responded to his desire to rebuild the walls of Jerusalem with passion, strength, courage, leadership, confidence, and integrity. What have your *starting blocks* required of you? List a few of the words and write a brief sentence about how you had to exercise those words as you got started on something big or new.

Read 2 Peter 1:2–4. Pay attention to verse 3, where Peter states that God has given you everything you need to lead a godly life—including the momentum you need to get out of the starting blocks. Close your time in prayer by thanking God for past opportunities you've been given to start something new, something big, or something hard—and ask God for whatever you need in your current season to get out of the starting blocks.

THE BEST APPROACH

Nehemiah wasn't interested in just getting *started* with rebuilding the walls of ancient Jerusalem. He wanted to get started *right*—and to do this, he had to consider the best approach to tackle the situation. For Nehemiah, this involved making an honest evaluation of the problem, identifying with the need of his people, taking personal responsibility for his part, and moving out of his comfort zones. Nehemiah thus gives us a *thoughtful approach* and a *helpful framework* for starting something new in our lives. Take a few moments to likewise reflect on your own approach to rebuilding as you respond to the following questions.

1 Consider an area or broken piece of your life where you
need a small or large amount of rebuilding (*losing weight,
rebuilding a relationship, switching gears with a ministry
opportunity*). What has been your approach so far to
rebuilding those broken places?

2 When it comes to addressing problems, many of us adopt
one of three approaches:

- **Superficial optimism**: We put a positive spin on our
  difficult situations, often pretending the problem
  does not exist.
- **Busy optimism:** We attack the problem by diving
  into work and busyness and develop all things "new"
  as a distraction from the problem—new policies, new
  plans, new people, and the like.
- **Honest optimism:** We seek to address the issue with
  wisdom, understanding, strength, and patience, and
  actually work to correct the issue.

Which of these approaches do you typically take when
faced with a problem? What has been the result of responding in that manner?

3 Why do you think you've responded this way? What, if anything, is keeping you from responding as the honest optimist?

4 Now consider some of the roadblocks that are currently getting in the way of your rebuilding process. What are the top three to five things that are keeping you from rebuilding (*problems, mindsets, people, processes*)?

5 Now use Nehemiah's approach to assess your own rebuilding process. Begin with an honest evaluation. What facts do you need to face right now about the situation that needs rebuilding in your life?

6 Nehemiah identified with the needs of his people. He wept, mourned, fasted, and prayed for days. He considered the pain and the distress of his people and allowed himself to feel their pain. How do you feel about this area of your life that needs rebuilding? What is hard or painful about the situation?

How does this situation affect the people around you? What have you noticed about their responses to this scenario?

What is hopeful about this situation?

7 How are you taking personal responsibility for this situation? Notice the moments where you may have placed blame on others by using the term "they." In what ways can you start taking personal and collective responsibility by saying, "I" and "we"?

8 Is there a comfort zone (or two) that you need to move out of in order to focus on the rebuilding process? If so, list those below, and then write down one or two steps you will you take to move out of them as you begin rebuilding.

My comfort zones:

Steps I will to take to move out of these comfort zones:

Read John 1:1–14. Jesus left the "comfort zone" of heaven to identify with our plight and provide a way to rebuild our broken relationship with God. He became one of us and made His dwelling among us—and because of this, you can be sure that He understands what you are facing in this life. Close your time in prayer by thanking God for Jesus—the ultimate rebuilder—and for the thoughtful approach to rebuilding our lives that we see in the life of Nehemiah. Ask God to give you the wisdom and insight to rebuild in this way as well.

SERVE THE KING

Nehemiah briefly mentions his status by saying, "I was the king's cupbearer" (Nehemiah 1:11). In ancient Persia, this meant he was the most trusted confidant of the king of the most powerful nation on earth. He was constantly by the king's side. There was no greater role for Nehemiah, the exiled Israelite, to hold in ancient Persia. And yet he left this prized role to rebuild the walls of Jerusalem. He left the service of one king for the service of *the* King.

From the outside looking in, Nehemiah's decision likely did not make sense to the people around him. But Nehemiah knew, with strength and conviction, that rebuilding the wall was what he needed to do. Consider the times when this has been true in your own life as you reflect on the following questions.

1. How can you identify with Nehemiah's decision to leave the kingdom of Persia behind and begin rebuilding the wall in Jerusalem? Has there ever been a time when you sensed God asking you to leave something behind to pursue a new task or vision?

2. If so, what was that like for you? What did the people around you think or say about your decision?

3. Consider the area of life you are currently rebuilding. What brought you to the point of deciding to rebuild this particular area, situation, or relationship?

4. Have there been moments when rebuilding didn't seem to "make sense"? If so, what keeps you moving forward, or what keeps you wanting to move forward, in this area?

5. How does your relationship with God motivate or influence the rebuilding process in your life?

6 How does the idea of considering God's presence in your everyday life change the way you view the areas of your life that need rebuilding?

7 What do you sense God saying to you at this moment about the area of your life that needs rebuilding or is in process?

8 What has been your response to God? (Remember, there is no right or wrong way to respond to God. God already knows what is on your heart and your mind, but He longs to hear your thoughts in conversation as well.)

Read Psalm 119:15, 59. In these verses, the psalmist writes about *considering the ways* of God. We see Nehemiah doing the same in the passage we've studied this week. Close your time in prayer today by thanking God for being near to you as you embrace the area of your life where you need to rebuild. Ask God to give you the willingness to consider His ways as you rebuild, even when they may not make sense to the world around you.

MODERN-DAY NEHEMIAH

Is there a modern-day Nehemiah in your world? Someone who has rebuilt from the rubble of their life—a relationship, business, team, idea, church or ministry, his or her own physical health? If so, ask that person to share more of his or her story with you. If you can't think of anyone in close proximity, find a podcast or read a book about someone who has rebuilt something. Either way, find a few people who inspire you with their stories, like Nehemiah, as you get started right on your new beginning. Write down some names that come to mind.

For Next Week: Review chapters 1–4 in *The Nehemiah Code* and use the space below to write any insights or questions from your personal study that you want to discuss at the next group meeting. In preparation for next week, review chapters 5–9 in *The Nehemiah Code.*

BUILD A TEAM SPIRIT
Nehemiah 2:1–20

The ability to work together and not against one another is an essential element of rebuilding. This is true whether we are seeking to rebuild a life, a business, a church, an athletic team, a marriage, self-confidence, or whatever. . . . The most successful homes are built by families who play together as a team. The most successful businesses are those in which every employee is valued, and they all work together as a team. Getting started right may be essential, but building a team spirit is what adds fuel to the rebuilding process.

O.S. HAWKINS

WELCOME

At just over 550 feet, the Washington Monument is the world's tallest predominantly stone structure.[1] Constructed of marble, granite, and bluestone gneiss, it stands out among the other tourist attractions in Washington, DC.[2] More than half a million people visit the monument each year.[3] But what few realize is that it would likely have never been finished were it not for the unique skills of an engineer named Thomas Lincoln Casey.

Originally, the project had fallen under the direction of the Washington National Monument Society, who collected donations and held a competition in 1836 for its design. Construction began in 1848 but came to an abrupt halt in 1856 due to a lack of funds, support, and direction.[4] At that time, a group known as the Know-Nothing Party seized control of the project, prompting Congress to suspend further contributions. For the next twenty years the monument sat untouched, until Casey was hired in 1878 to complete the job.[5]

After carefully analyzing the situation, Casey discovered the structure was leaning to the northwest due a faulty foundation. So he quickly set goals for the project, seized the opportunity to make changes, and hired a team of workers. Together, they came up with a plan for balancing the foundation as laborers dug from either side in a coordinated effort.[6] Eventually, the team repaired the faulty foundation, and work was completed in 1888.[7]

In Ecclesiastes 4:12 we read, "Though one may be over-powered by another, two can withstand him. And a threefold cord is not quickly broken." When it comes to rebuilding, we can't go it alone. As we will see today, while getting started right is essential, building a team spirit is what adds fuel to the process and keeps it moving toward a successful completion.

SHARE

If you or any of your group members are just meeting for the first time, take a few minutes to introduce yourselves and share any insights you have from last week's personal study. Next, to kick things off for the group time, discuss one of the following questions:

- What is the best team you have been a part of? What are some of the characteristics of that team that made it so great?

—or—

- When have you seen teamwork pay off in your life? How have you found that working with others has been beneficial to you?

READ

Invite someone to read aloud the following passage. Listen for fresh insight and share any new thoughts with the group through the questions that follow.

And it came to pass in the month of Nisan, in the twentieth year of King Artaxerxes, when wine was before him, that I took the wine and gave it to the king. Now I had never been sad in his presence before. Therefore the king said to me, "Why is your face sad, since you are not sick? This is nothing but sorrow of heart."

So I became dreadfully afraid, and said to the king, "May the king live forever! Why should my face not be sad, when the city, the place of my fathers' tombs, lies waste, and its gates are burned with fire?"

Then the king said to me, "What do you request?"

So I prayed to the God of heaven. And I said to the king, "If it pleases the king, and if your servant has found favor in your sight, I ask that you send me to Judah, to the city of my fathers' tombs, that I may rebuild it." . . .

Furthermore I said to the king, "If it pleases the king, let letters be given to me for the governors of the region beyond the River, that they must permit me to pass through till I come to Judah, and a letter to Asaph the keeper of the king's forest, that he must give me timber to make beams for the gates of the citadel which pertains to the temple, for the city wall, and for the house that I will occupy." And the king granted them to me according to the good hand of my God upon me.

Then I went to the governors in the region beyond the River, and gave them the king's letters. Now the king had sent captains of the army and horsemen with me. . . . .

So I came to Jerusalem and was there three days. Then I arose in the night, I and a few men with me; I told no one what my God had put in my heart to do at Jerusalem; nor was there any animal with me, except the one on which I rode. And I went out by night through the Valley Gate to the Serpent Well and the Refuse Gate, and viewed the walls of Jerusalem which were broken down and its gates which were burned with fire. . . .

Then I said to them, "You see the distress that we are in, how Jerusalem lies waste, and its gates are burned with fire. Come and let us build the wall of Jerusalem, that we may no longer be a reproach." And I told them of the hand of my God which had been good upon me, and also of the king's words that he had spoken to me.

So they said, "Let us rise up and build." Then they set their hands to this good work.

But when Sanballat the Horonite, Tobiah the Ammonite official, and Geshem the Arab heard of it, they laughed at us and despised us, and said, "What is this thing that you are doing? Will you rebel against the king?"

So I answered them, and said to them, "The God of heaven Himself will prosper us; therefore we His servants will arise and build, but you have no heritage or right or memorial in Jerusalem" (Nehemiah 2:1–5, 7–9, 11–13, 17–20).

◆ What is one key insight that stands out to you from this passage?

◆ What steps did Nehemiah take to *build a team spirit* when he saw the state of the walls?

WATCH

Play the video for session two. As you and your group watch, use the following outline to record any thoughts or key points that stand out to you.

Notes

Rebuilders are wise enough to know that synergy is vitally important in the rebuilding process.

Step 1 in building a team spirit is to *start with your goal in mind*. Nehemiah demonstrated this by . . .

Step 2 in building a team spirit is to *seize your opportunity*. Nehemiah demonstrated this by . . .

Step 3 in building a team spirit is to make *a careful analysis of the situation*. Nehemiah demonstrated this by . . .

Step 4 in building a team spirit is to motivate *people to get off a dead center*. Nehemiah was able to motivate his people to act in the following stages . . .

- Conception:

- Gestation

- Adoption

- Maturity

Step 5 in building a team spirit is to *stay on track*. Nehemiah demonstrated this by . . .

DISCUSS

Take a few minutes with your group members to discuss what you just watched and explore these concepts together.

1 How would you define the word *synergy*? Why is the principle of synergy so important when it comes to the rebuilding process?

2 How did Nehemiah demonstrate that he had a plan for rebuilding the walls of Jerusalem? What tends to happen when people do not have clear and measurable goals for what they want to accomplish?

3 What did Nehemiah do to seize his opportunity of making his dream for rebuilding the walls come to pass? What are some of the opportunities that you've seized in life?

4 Why did Nehemiah feel it was necessary to ride out at night to survey the broken walls? How does having the facts of a situation help you to make better decisions?

5 How did Nehemiah show the people that his vision was conceivable, believable, and achievable? Why is this important if you want others to buy in to your vision?

6 What are some of the immediate obstacles that Nehemiah faced when the people started the work? How could his example help you to stay on track with your goals when you are presented with challenges and distractions?

RESPOND

Briefly review the outline for the video teaching and any notes you took. In the space below, write down the most significant point you took away from this session.

PRAY

End the gathering by partnering with another person from your group and, if you are comfortable in doing so, briefly share a vision or goal that you are pursuing. Pray that God would bring clarity to the other person's situation and help him or her to seize the opportunities presented, move forward, and not get off track. Write down any specific requests in the space below so you can remember to continue praying throughout the week.

BETWEEN-SESSIONS PERSONAL STUDY

*R*ebuilders know that when it comes to taking the next step toward a goal, it is vitally important to have the support and encouragement of their friends and family if they want to succeed. So this week, take the next step in your rebuilding process by spending some time with God each day and engaging in any or all of the following activities. Be sure to read the reflection questions after each activity and make a few notes in your guide about the experience. At the start of the next session you will have a few minutes to share any insights you learned.

REMEMBER THE PAST

Getting started with the rebuilding process can be difficult. We procrastinate. We get distracted. We are reminded of our failures. We make statements like "that will never happen" or "I can't do that." We struggle with the idea of dealing with the rubble in our lives.

Perhaps this is why Nehemiah stresses that a key to the rebuilding process—whether you are rebuilding a business, a relationship, a church or ministry, or pieces of your life—is building *team spirit*. But building this team spirit starts with you . . . and in particular, it starts with having *your goal in mind*. Often, you can gain confidence for pursuing a present goal by remembering the past victories that you have attained. With this in mind, take a few minutes to reflect on your past successes as you respond to the following questions.

1   Think a time when you tackled a challenging rebuilding project. What was it? Write down a few examples and mark the example that is most clear to you.

2   What goals did you have in mind at the start of that project?

3   What opportunities did you seize that built momentum for the situation?

4   How did you carefully analyze the situation?

5 How did you motivate the people involved in the process with you?

6 How did you stay focused on your goals?

7 Who were the critical voices weighing in on your project or process? How did you respond to those voices?

8 What was the outcome of this rebuilding experience? How did you feel about the outcome and about yourself as a result of the experience?

Read Matthew 4:18–22. Consider how the disciples committed to rebuilding their lives by following Jesus. Also consider how Jesus seized the opportunity to invite the disciples to follow Him while they were in the middle of working. Think about your own past rebuilding experience and thank God for the lessons you learned. Ask God today to show you what lessons to carry with you and what to let go of from the past as you move forward.

NOTICE THE PRESENT

Consider the project you are working on rebuilding right now, or the rebuilding process you need to get started right now. Use the questions below to get started.

1 How would you describe the project, process, or situation you are working to rebuild?

2 What goals do you have in mind for this project? (Pick three to five goals and start there. Having more than five goals may seem out of reach in the beginning.)

3 What current opportunities do you have to seize?

4 How will you take careful analysis of the situation?

5 What will you do to motivate the people involved in the process with you?

6 How will you stay focused with your goals?

7 Who are the critical voices weighing in on your project? How do you plan to respond to those voices?

8 What are your hopes and dreams for this rebuilding? In two to four sentences, relate the story of how this rebuilding project will make life better for you and those involved.

Read Matthew 9:20–21. Consider the woman who reached out for healing. Even though she had been bleeding for years, she seized the *present moment* to be healed by Jesus. Now consider the lessons you are learning from your *present* rebuilding experience. Thank God for those lessons and ask Him to continually show you how to move forward.

GET MOTIVATED

When building a team spirit, it is critical to *motivate the people involved to get off dead center*. Remember your high school coach, energetic youth pastor, or office cheerleader? We're talking about *that* kind of motivation. But you can't just shout out motivational encouragements to get people moving—you need the right goals and attitude. In this regard, there are at least three rules of goal-setting to keep in mind when seeking to motivate your people:

1. **Conception:** The goal must be *conceivable*. It is vital for those around to envision the plan of where you are going and how you are going to get there.
2. **Adoption:** The goal must be *adoptable*. Establish goals that people can really believe will be accomplished.
3. **Achievable:** The goal must be *attainable*. The goals need to be within reach of what the people can actually do.

There are also four attitudes you need to possess to motivate others:

1. **Face Up:** Deal with the issue at hand and don't blame others.
2. **Team Up:** Realize that you need others and they need you.
3. **Gird Up:** Get off the couch and begin to work on the issue at hand. Accept the fact that life goes on and start placing one building stone upon another.

4. **Look Up:** Remember it is never too late for a new beginning, no matter who you are or where you are in life.

Keep these points in mind as you use the following questions to define your own goals and helpful attitudes to build a team spirit.

1 Consider the three rules of goal-setting as they relate to your current rebuilding project. Are your goals conceivable for those around you? If so, in what ways?

2 Are your goals adoptable? How do you know? What response have you received from others about whether they are attainable?

3 Are your goals achievable? If so, in what ways? (If you're uncertain, ask the people involved in the process with you to help answer this question.)

4 Now consider the four attitudes for motivating others. Where do you need to face up and deal with the real issue at hand? Be honest with yourself. How have you been blaming someone or something else?

5 How can you team up with the people around you? Who is on your "team"—a coworker, a spouse, a friend, your pastor, a mentor, or a counselor? How will you include these individuals in your rebuilding process?

6 What is the most important thing you can do to gird up? Do you need to get off the couch and actually start working on your goals today? Do you need to seize an opportunity, have a direct conversation with someone, or make a difficult decision? List what you need to do and how you will accomplish that task this week.

7 How will you look up today? What do you need to hear right now in regard to your rebuilding project?

8 Out of everything you wrote down or thought about today, consider where you need the most inspiration or motivation. Is it *facing up, teaming up, girding up,* or *looking up?* Or is it in making your goals *conceivable, believable,* and *achievable?* Explain.

Read Isaiah 30:21. Consider where you need the most inspiration and motivation as you build team spirit in your rebuilding process, and invite God into that process. Remember that He will show you the way if you pay attention. Thank Him today for the people who are a part of your rebuilding experience and for the people who will be a part of it in the future. Also ask God to show you the single most important step you can take right now to move forward.

STAY FOCUSED

For some of us, getting started isn't the hard part . . . it's *staying focused* that's the problem. It's perhaps true to say that we have more distractions in our modern-day world than Nehemiah had back in his day. But Nehemiah's ability to *stay focused* remains a necessary and steady model for rebuilding even in our modern-day world. As we learn from his example, there are four keys to staying focused as we work to build a team spirit:

1. Keep your eyes on Jesus and your faith in God
2. Develop a servant's heart
3. Get busy with the task
4. See our critics for what they are

Think about another "modern-day" Nehemiah in your life who has had success in building a team spirit. Look for someone who has invited a team of people into his or her life for support, collaboration, and accountability. This could be a couple who sought the support of a counselor or pastor while they were going through a rough patch in their relationship. Or a leader who invited her team's perspective and people on the "outside" to give their ideas during a challenging season. Or a pastor who was willing to heed the cautions of his board members when they said he might be on the brink of a burnout.

Whoever you choose, ask this person how he or she managed to stay focused during that time. What lessons did the person learn to staying focused? What would he or she do all over again or do differently next time? Consider which lessons you could apply to your own experience and write these ideas below.

For Next Week: Use the space below to write any key insights or questions from your personal study that you want to discuss at the next group meeting. In preparation for next week, review chapters 10–14 in *The Nehemiah Code.*

Three

LET GO WITHOUT LETTING UP

Nehemiah 3:1–29

Many people who start out with big dreams of rebuilding never see their wall completed because they have never discovered the art of delegation. Quite honestly, a lot of us confuse "delegate" with "dictate" or "abdicate". . . . I have observed some pastors who are so overwhelmed they begin to dictate to others and others who simply abdicated. But the wise leader is the one who learns the art of delegation and puts it into practice, who knows how to let things go to other people, but who doesn't let up on the accountability factor.

O.S. HAWKINS

WELCOME

Andrew Carnegie is best known as being a dogged industrialist who singlehandedly built the steel industry in the United States from the ground up. Born in Scotland, he immigrated to America at a young age with his impoverished family. A true rags-to-riches story, he started his career as a "bobbin boy"— changing spools of thread in a cotton mill—at a meager wage of $1.20 per week.[1] By the end of his life, he was considered one of the richest men in the world.[2]

Carnegie had a strong work ethic and knew how to hustle to get what he wanted. But over the course of his life, he had also discovered the fine art of delegating authority—and he wasn't shy about telling others they needed to work *smarter* instead of *harder*.[3] One time, a friend bragged that he arrived to work at seven in the morning and stayed until late. Carnegie replied, "You must be a lazy man if it takes you ten hours to do a day's work. What I do is get good men, and I never give them orders. . . . In the morning I get reports from them. Within an hour I have disposed of everything, sent out all my suggestions, the day's work done."[4]

King Solomon wrote, "Two are better than one, because they have a good reward for their labor" (Ecclesiastes 4:9). When it comes to rebuilding, we can't go it alone . . . but neither can we dictate to others or abdicate our responsibilities. Rebuilding requires us to let go of the control while remaining focused and driven on achieving the end goal. As we will see today, this was a concept that Nehemiah had grasped. He let go, but he never let up.

SHARE

Begin your group time by inviting anyone to share his or her insights from last week's personal study. Next, to kick things off, discuss one of the following questions:

- What are some of the challenges you face when it comes to delegating responsibilities to others? What helps you to let go of the need for control?

—or—

- Why is it difficult to work with people who are dictators? Why is it difficult to work with people who are always abdicating their responsibilities to others?

READ

Invite two people to read aloud the following passages. Listen for fresh insight and to share any new thoughts with the group through the questions that follow.

Then Eliashib the high priest rose up with his brethren the priests and built the Sheep Gate; they consecrated it and hung its doors. They built as far as the Tower of the Hundred, and consecrated it, then as far as the Tower of

Hananel. Next to Eliashib the men of Jericho built. And next to them Zaccur the son of Imri built.

Also the sons of Hassenaah built the Fish Gate; they laid its beams and hung its doors with its bolts and bars. And next to them Meremoth the son of Urijah, the son of Koz, made repairs. Next to them Meshullam the son of Berechiah, the son of Meshezabel, made repairs. Next to them Zadok the son of Baana made repairs. Next to them the Tekoites made repairs; but their nobles did not put their shoulders to the work of their Lord. . . .

After him Baruch the son of Zabbai carefully repaired the other section, from the buttress to the door of the house of Eliashib the high priest. After him Meremoth the son of Urijah, the son of Koz, repaired another section, from the door of the house of Eliashib to the end of the house of Eliashib.

And after him the priests, the men of the plain, made repairs. After him Benjamin and Hasshub made repairs opposite their house. After them Azariah the son of Maaseiah, the son of Ananiah, made repairs by his house. . . .

Beyond the Horse Gate the priests made repairs, each in front of his own house (Nehemiah 3:1–5, 20–23, 28).

◆ What is one key insight that stands out to you from this passage?

♦ What does this passage reveal about the way in which the work was distributed?

WATCH

Play the video for session three. As you and your group watch, use the following outline to record any thoughts or key points that stand out to you.

Notes

Nehemiah shows us the importance of delegation in the rebuilding task—of enlisting other people to help us in our tasks.

Step 1 in letting go without letting up is to *set clear objectives with specific tasks*. Nehemiah demonstrated this by . . .

Step 2 in letting go without letting up is to *pick the right person for the right job*. Nehemiah demonstrated this by . . .

Step 3 in letting go without letting up is to *be an example yourself.* Nehemiah demonstrated this by . . .

Step 4 in letting go without letting up is to *hold people accountable.* Nehemiah demonstrated this by . . .

Step 5 in letting go without letting up is to *give genuine pats on the back.* Nehemiah demonstrated this by . . .

DISCUSS

Take a few minutes with your group members to discuss what you just watched and explore these concepts together.

1   What does it mean to "let go without letting up"? Why is it often difficult to navigate the path between too much control (dictating) and not enough control (abdicating)?

2 How did Nehemiah divide up the work among the people? What does his example reveal about the need to have clear tasks and objectives?

3 Why did Nehemiah choose some of the people to make the repairs in front of their own homes? What are some methods you use to pick the right person for the right job?

4 What did Nehemiah do to show that he was a worker right alongside the people? Why is it critical for you to be a good example for others in your own rebuilding efforts?

5 Nehemiah knew which people were responsible for building each section of the wall. Why was this necessary? How do you tend to hold others responsible for tasks?

6 What are some of the ways that Nehemiah encouraged the workers? What is a recent time that someone gave you encouragement for a job well done?

RESPOND

Briefly review the outline for the video teaching and any notes you took. In the space below, write down the most significant point you took away from this session.

PRAY

End the gathering by partnering with one or two people from your group and praying for each another. Pray especially that God would help you surrender control of your lives to Him and that He would give you opportunities to encourage others. Write down any specific requests in the space below so you can remember to continue praying throughout the week.

BETWEEN-SESSIONS PERSONAL STUDY

*R*ebuilders understand that when it comes to working with others toward a common goal, they need to be *delegators* rather than *dictators* or *abdicators*. This week, spend some time with God each day to explore this topic in the Bible as you engage in any or all of the following activities. Be sure to read the reflection questions and make a few notes that you can share at the next group meeting.

ART OF DELEGATION

A key secret to Nehemiah's success as a leader was his ability to delegate. In our own lives, no matter what we are attempting to rebuild, learning to delegate tasks and responsibilities—by *letting go without letting up*—will likewise be a key to our success. Delegation is an important means by which we should complete the work we set out to accomplish.

But sometimes, it's easy to *dictate* instead of delegate—to get bogged down in every little detail of the process. We may even convince ourselves it's *best* if we stay in control of every piece. Other times, it's easy to fall into the trap of *abdicating* instead of delegating—by giving up all our control to other people. This often occurs when we feel uncertain of our own abilities to lead . . . but we abdicate at the cost of giving up our voice in the effort.

Delegation requires a medium between the two extremes. And, as we find in the Bible, the best leaders know how to walk this line well between dictating and abdicating. Today, consider your own leadership style and the way you "let go without letting up" as you reflect on the following examples from the lives of Moses, Nehemiah, and Jesus.

1   Read Exodus 18. Why did Jethro say to Moses, "The thing that you do is not good" (verse 17)? What changes did Moses make as a result of Jethro's advice?

2   If Jethro appeared in your life today, is there any area of your leadership where he would say, "The thing that you do is not good"? What specific tasks or responsibilities could you be delegating instead of holding onto right now?

3   Reread Nehemiah 3. What does this chapter tell you about Nehemiah's style of delegating? How does this encourage you as you reflect on your own delegation style?

4   Read John 6:1–14 and Luke 9:10–16. In each of these accounts of Jesus feeding the 5,000, how did He delegate responsibilities to His disciples?

5   What in these stories stands out to you or relates to you personally?

6   Delegating allows you to be the best version of yourself as a leader and allows your projects and processes to reach their fullest potential. What are some examples of the healthy delegation you've witnessed from leaders around you? How did their delegation influence their people and their projects?

7   If you have a hard time delegating tasks and responsibilities, think about why this might be a challenge for you. Do you lean more toward dictating, where you prefer to remain in control, or abdicating, where you completely let go? Why?

8 Learning the art of delegating is the key to success. Many people start out with big dreams of rebuilding but never see their "wall" completed because they refuse to embrace the art of delegating. What specific steps can you take today to start delegating tasks and responsibilities as it relates to your rebuilding project?

Read Galatians 6:4–6. Delegating might look different for each of us because we've been wired in different ways. Yet God gives us the freedom to discover the unique ways we've been created, and He gives us opportunities to bring our best to the rebuilding process—for our own good and the common good of those around us. Close today by thanking God for the way He's wired you and for the opportunities He's given you to learn the art of delegation.

FIVE PRINCIPLES OF DELEGATION

When you look at Nehemiah's life and leadership style, it is clear to see that he was skilled in the art of delegating. As you dig deeper, you will find that there were actually five important principles he followed in dividing out tasks among the people. These "five principles of delegation" could be summed up as follows:

1. Set clear objectives with specific tasks
2. Pick the right person for the right job
3. Set an example yourself

4. Hold people accountable
5. Give genuine "pats on the back"

Take a few moments to consider how you employ these five principles in your own rebuilding efforts as you respond to the following questions.

1 What clear objectives with specific tasks do you set when you assign tasks to others?

2 How do you determine which person to pick for which job? Have you ever picked the *wrong* person for a job? If so, what steps did you take to fix the problem?

3 How are you setting an example? What are a few specific actions, behaviors, and conversations you've had that set the example for how you expect others to behave when they are working with you?

4   How are you holding people accountable? (Setting clear
    objectives ahead of time will help with holding people
    accountable. Instead of having hard conversations
    about your own personal preferences, the accountability
    comes when you can point back to guiding principles or
    expectations set at the beginning of the project.)

5   What does it look like for you to give people a genuine
    "pat on the back"? (Keep in mind that this may look
    different for various members of your team. Some people
    need an actual pat on the back, others need words of
    encouragement, some need to be acknowledged for their
    contribution in front of their peers. Figure out what it
    looks like to give your people a genuine "pat on the back"
    and make it a regular habit.)

6   Consider the five principles of delegation. Using a scale
    from 1–10, with 1 being least effective and 10 being the
    most effective, how would you rate your ability to live out
    these principles? Why?

7 Which principle do you need to work on the most? How will you do this?

8 Which principle are you succeeding at the most? In what ways?

Read Galatians 6:1–2. Paul says that we are to carry each other's burdens. However, it's often difficult to let others know we are struggling and need help. Today, ask God to show you what it looks like to delegate authority and responsibilities in your life. Thank Him for the ways He has delegated His authority, wisdom, and love to you, and for the ways He has taken care of what you've already delegated to others.

INFLUENCE OF DELEGATION

Go back to the five principles of delegation for a moment. The second principle highlights the fact that Nehemiah knew how to pick the right person for the right job. But delegating isn't just about picking the right person. It's also about using our *influence*.

That word *influence* comes from two words in Latin, "in" and "flow."[5] Picture a mighty river that's flowing deep and clear with a strong current. Now picture all the little creeks, tributaries, and streams that flow into the river. When these smaller streams reach the mighty river, they get carried away in its flow. That's the idea behind the term *influence*.

The Bible says that we are to live our lives in such a godly manner that other people will be carried away in our flow. They move with us, instead of against us, because of the strong and clear current of our actions, behaviors, and words. Keep this idea in mind as you answer the following questions related to our influence as members of God's team.

1 What does *influence* mean to you?

2 The imagery of a mighty river "in flow" is a good description of our influence. What other images or ideas come to mind when you think of the word *influence*?

3 How have you been influenced by others?

4 How have you influenced others?

5 Think about the modern-day Nehemiahs in your life. What stands out to you about the ways they use their influence? What have you learned by watching them?

6 Consider your own rebuilding project. How have you used your influence in that specific project or process to get where you are right now?

7 Is there an area in your life, specifically as it relates to rebuilding, where it would be helpful to you and to the people around you if you exercised your influence more often?

8 Keep in mind that your influence isn't meant for you; it's meant for the common good of the world around you. How does this reminder change the way you use your influence?

Read 2 Corinthians 10:12–15. In these verses, Paul reminds us that God has assigned us to a sphere of influence. Today, ask God to give you the ability to see your current sphere of influence and the courage to use His authority to build others up in that sphere. Thank Him for the influence and opportunities you've been given to build others up in truth and lead well.

AFFIRMATION OF DELEGATION

The final principle of delegation refers to the idea that Nehemiah knew when to give his colaborers a genuine *pat on the back*. In other words, Nehemiah was good at giving affirmation when it was well-deserved. He went up and down the lines of people as they were rebuilding, stopping at each one, telling them they were doing a good job, and calling them out.

Affirmation means "showing or expressing a strong belief in someone" or "giving someone the emotional support and encouragement they need."[6] Of course, if we aren't used to *receiving* affirmation, we may have a hard time *giving* it to others. This is why we need to be intentional in this important principle of delegation if we want our rebuilding efforts to succeed. With this in mind, reflect on your own story as you respond to the following questions.

1 In what ways have you been affirmed in your own life?

2 Consider the affirmation you need to give to both *yourself* and to *others*. If affirmation has been lacking in your own life—either from your parents, your caregivers, your coaches, your boss, or your significant other—what words of affirmation do you wish you could hear from these important people in your life?

3 Who needs to hear words of affirmation from you? What do they need to hear you say?

Share this affirmation with these individuals sometime this week—in person, over the phone, via text, in an email response, or in front of their peers.

For Next Week: Use the space below to write any key insights or questions from your personal study that you want to discuss at the next group meeting. In preparation for next week, review chapters 15–18 in *The Nehemiah Code.*

Four

PERSEVERE THROUGH DIFFICULTIES

Nehemiah 4:1–23

Some of us never rebuild in life because as soon as we are hit with opposition, we are prone to quit, fumble away our opportunity, or, worse yet, start running in the opposite direction. But rebuilders always keep moving forward after they are hit because they have learned that it is the yards after contact that matter most in life. Often, yards after contact is what determines whether or not we reach our goal, and it is the key element that separates those who rebuild from those who don't.

O.S. HAWKINS

WELCOME

It is a sad fact of life that whenever you set out to create something good, there will be those who try to discourage you and criticize your work. Back in 1943, architect Frank Lloyd Wright found this to be true when he was commissioned to build a museum of art in the heart of New York City. The museum would come to be known as The Guggenheim, which to this day remains one of the most famous of Wright's many buildings.

When Wright was selected for the project, the only stipulation he was given was that "the building should be unlike any other museum in the world." Wright delivered by drafting plans for a round-shaped building that resembled—depending on who you ask—either a nautilus shell, concrete ribbon, or inverted ziggurat. To say it stood out among the surrounding buildings would be an understatement. And not everyone approved.

When the plans first reached the municipal authorities in 1952, they cited thirty-two building violations against it. Those issues were resolved by 1956, but as construction got underway a group of key artists sent a letter to the foundation to try to stop the building, stating it was "not suitable for a sympathetic display of painting and sculpture." Fortunately, the foundation persevered, and today The Guggenheim has become one of the most popular museums in New York, attracting around a million visitors each year.[1]

Jesus said that "in the world you will have tribulation" (John 16:33), and often that trouble will come at the hands of those who want to derail your efforts at rebuilding. However, as Nehemiah demonstrates, there is a way to deal with obstacles and keep pressing forward. Today, we will see how he was able to persevere in spite of very real threats against his people.

SHARE

Begin your group time by inviting anyone to share his or her insights from last week's personal study. Next, to kick things off, discuss one of the following questions:

- What are some of the reasons why a person might try to derail another person's efforts? How have you seen this play out in the media lately?

—*or*—

- How do you tend to react when you face opposition? Is there anything that you would like to change in the way you react?

READ

Invite someone to read aloud the following passage. Listen for fresh insight and share any new thoughts with the group through the questions that follow.

But it so happened, when Sanballat heard that we were rebuilding the wall, that he was furious and very indignant, and mocked the Jews. And he spoke before his brethren and the army of Samaria, and said, "What are these feeble Jews doing? Will they fortify themselves? Will they offer sacrifices? Will they complete it in a day? Will they revive the stones from the heaps of rubbish—stones that are burned?". . .

So we built the wall, and the entire wall was joined together up to half its height, for the people had a mind to work.

Now it happened, when Sanballat, Tobiah, the Arabs, the Ammonites, and the Ashdodites heard that the walls of Jerusalem were being restored and the gaps were beginning to be closed, that they became very angry, and all of them conspired together to come and attack Jerusalem and create confusion. Nevertheless we made our prayer to our God, and because of them we set a watch against them day and night.

Then Judah said, "The strength of the laborers is failing, and there is so much rubbish that we are not able to build the wall."

And our adversaries said, "They will neither know nor see anything, till we come into their midst and kill them and cause the work to cease."

So it was, when the Jews who dwelt near them came, that they told us ten times, "From whatever place you turn, they will be upon us."

Therefore I positioned men behind the lower parts of the wall, at the openings; and I set the people according to their families, with their swords, their spears, and their bows. And I looked, and arose and said to the nobles, to the *leaders, and to the rest of the people, "Do not be afraid of them. Remember the Lord, great and awesome, and fight for your brethren, your sons, your daughters, your wives, and your houses."...*

Then I said to the nobles, the rulers, and the rest of the people, "The work is great and extensive, and we are separated far from one another on the wall. Wherever you hear the sound of the trumpet, rally to us there. Our God will fight for us" (Nehemiah 4:1–2, 6–14, 19–20).

◆ What was one thing that stood out to you from the Scripture?

◆ How did Nehemiah react when his enemies tried to discourage him? How did he react when his enemies picked up weapons to attack the people?

WATCH

Play the video for session four. As you and your group watch, use the following outline to record any thoughts or key points that stand out to you.

Notes

Sometimes the wind is against us . . . and how we overcome obstacles will determine the rebuilding process for us.

When we're rebuilding our lives, we should expect opposition. If we don't meet opposition, it could be that we're going the same way the devil is going!

Step 1 in persevering through difficulties is to *deal with conflict head on.*

- Nehemiah dealt with opposition from the *outside* by . . .

- Nehemiah dealt with opposition from the *inside* by . . .

Step 2 in persevering through difficulties is to *make the proper adjustments.* Nehemiah demonstrated this by . . .

Step 3 in persevering through difficulties is to *keep doing what is right.* Nehemiah demonstrated this by . . .

Step 4 in persevering through difficulties is to *rally the troops.* Nehemiah demonstrated this by . . .

DISCUSS

Take a few minutes with your group members to discuss what
you just watched and explore these concepts together.

1 In football, "yards after contact" refers to the yards a
player gains after being hit by the opposing team. How
does this apply to life? Why is it important to keep
moving forward when you are faced with opposition?

2 How did Nehemiah deal with the outside threat from
Sanballat, Tobiah, and the others? What are some
ways that the enemy has tried to attack your self-worth
and morale?

3 How did Nehemiah deal with the inside threat from
his own people? When have you seen *fatigue* lead to
frustration and then *failure*?

4 In what way did Nehemiah respond to the complaints
   from Judah that there was too much rubble in the way
   to rebuild the wall? When are some times that the task
   seemed daunting to you . . . and you had to make some
   adjustments to your thinking?

5 How did Nehemiah continue to protect his people as
   the opposition intensified? How do you stay focused on
   doing what is right when faced with a crisis?

6 What did Nehemiah do to rally the troops? Who has
   been an important encourager in your life? How has that
   person helped you?

RESPOND

Briefly review the outline for the video teaching and any notes you took. In the space below, write down the most significant point you took away from this session.

PRAY

End the gathering by partnering with another person from your group and, if you are comfortable in doing so, briefly share a challenge or obstacle that you are facing. Pray that God would help the other person to persevere during that difficulty and give him or her clarity on the next steps to take. Write down any specific requests in the space below so you can remember to continue praying throughout the week.

BETWEEN-SESSIONS PERSONAL STUDY

*R*ebuilders recognize that at some point in their journey—if they are truly following God's will—they will face opposition. This week, spend some time in God's Word and explore what steps He says you should take when faced with trials. Be sure to read the reflection questions after each activity and make a few notes in your guide about the experience. At the start of the next session you will have a few minutes to share any insights you learned.

DEAL WITH THE CONFLICT

Conflict resolution is a hot topic these days, in both the business world and the social arena. Conflict can tear a team apart—whether it is in the home, at the office, on the court, or even in the church. Fortunately, Nehemiah's story gives us some helpful examples of how to successfully deal with the conflict that will come our way—and persevere through it.

When Nehemiah's enemies opposed the rebuilding efforts, his first response was to *deal with the conflict head-on*. In his case, this meant confronting the outward threat from the men who verbally attacked his people's *morale, motives,* and overall *mission*. But Nehemiah reveals that it is also important to deal with conflict head-on when it comes from the inside. In his case, this meant confronting the Jews' own internal *fatigue, frustration,* and sense of *failure*.

1 Reread Nehemiah 4. What stands out to you about the way Nehemiah dealt with the external opposition faced by the Jews?

2 What kind of external opposition have you faced recently as it relates to your rebuilding efforts? Or, if you're just getting started, what kind of external opposition do you anticipate you will face?

3 How have you responded in the past when others attacked your morale, your motives, or your mission?

4 Based on Nehemiah's example of dealing with conflict head-on, how do you hope to handle such external opposition in the future?

5 What stands out to you about the way Nehemiah dealt with the internal opposition he was faced with from the Jews?

6 What kind of internal opposition have you faced as it relates to your rebuilding efforts? Or, if you're just getting started, what kind of internal opposition do you anticipate?

7 How have you responded in the past when dealing with internal opposition such as fatigue, frustration, and failure?

8 Based on Nehemiah's example of dealing with conflict head-on, how do you hope to handle internal opposition in the future?

Read 1 Corinthians 9:1–18. In these verses, Paul provides us with an example from his own life on what it looks like to face internal conflict head-on. Close by asking God to show you how to respond to the opposition you are facing, and thank Him for the people in your life who are willing to journey with you even in the midst of that opposition. Also pray for those individuals and for the opposition that they are facing in their own lives.

MAKE PROPER ADJUSTMENTS

Nehemiah's second response when faced with opposition was to *make proper adjustments*. As repairs got underway, some of the people complained there was just too much rubble to remove—they wanted to leave the rubbish and build a wall on top of it. But Nehemiah was wise enough to know they had to remove the rubbish or the walls would crumble again.

In our own interactions, if we're not willing to go back to the foundation of our relationships and remove the rubbish— the junk and debris that inevitably comes—then we will have a hard time moving forward. Removing the rubbish in relationships often means being willing to say, "I'm sorry," and also being willing to extend forgiveness to others.

1 What have you learned from Nehemiah about making proper adjustments?

2 How have you applied this wisdom to your own rebuilding project? In what areas have you had to "remove rubbish" in order to keep rebuilding?

3 What was the rubbish you had to remove? And how did it get there?

4 How did the people who were with you in the rebuilding process respond to your decision to remove the rubbish?

5 Are there any other proper adjustments you need to make as you continue to rebuild?

6 Now consider your personal life. What proper adjustments need to be made? What kinds of rubbish need to be removed?

7 Removing the rubbish isn't as easy as it seems. Think of a friend, colleague, mentor, or teammate with whom you can share your list of "rubbish." How do you need them to hold you accountable as you take action to make changes in your life?

8 How will making proper adjustments and clearing away the rubbish allow you to rebuild from a better place or with better perspective?

Read John 2:13–22. In this passage, Jesus "cleared the rubbish" from the temple courts. He knew He had to take swift action for the temple to return to being a proper place of worship—and He did so by overturning the moneychangers' tables. Close today by asking God to give you the desire that is necessary to clear the rubbish from your own life. Thank Him for His presence as you take these hard steps of making proper adjustments in your rebuilding efforts.

KEEP DOING WHAT IS RIGHT

Nehemiah's third response when faced with opposition was to *keep doing what is right.* No matter who mocked him or questioned him or threatened him, he kept rebuilding the wall and never gave up. Nehemiah simply kept doing what was right. But we all know that doing what is right isn't always *that* simple. It takes strength, perseverance, courage, accountability, and a lot of hard work and vision to see the bigger picture.

1 What have you learned from Nehemiah about doing what is right?

2 What thoughts, feelings, or emotions do you think Nehemiah had in his quest to keep doing what is right?

3 How can you identify with Nehemiah in his efforts to always do what is right?

4 In what areas of your rebuilding project or process do you need to be reminded to keep doing what is right (*treating loved ones with respect, staying positive with your team, championing teammates who are quick to compete with you*)?

5 What makes it hard for you to do what is right in your current situation? List a few specific examples.

6 Sometimes you have to make things right before you can keep doing what is right. What needs to be made right in your life right now as you rebuild?

7   What has kept you from making things right up until this point?

8   What kind of encouragement do you need to hear from God, from your team, or from those closest to you to keep doing what is right?

Read Matthew 4:1–11. Sometimes we forget that Jesus had moments when He was faced with the decision to *keep doing what is right.* Today, think about how Jesus responded to temptation in this passage. Close by asking God to show you a few specific areas of your life where you need to keep doing what is right. Remember that God is with you every step of the way, and thank Him for the strength, courage, perseverance, and vision to keep doing what is right.

RALLY THE TROOPS

Nehemiah's fourth response when faced with opposition was to *rally the troops.* This means "to have a pep talk or boost morale, or to have a meeting where everyone stacks hands on an idea or decision."[2] Rallying the troops also means to unite a team around a common goal, vision, or idea. This is exactly what Nehemiah did at the end of chapter four in verses 18 through 20.

Nehemiah and the Jews were rebuilding more than two miles of broken walls around Jerusalem, and the people were scattered all across those walls. They were in their places, doing their jobs, and Nehemiah would rally them with the sound of a trumpet. He told the people, "Wherever you hear the sound of the trumpet, rally to us there. Our God will fight for us" (Nehemiah 4:20).

Maybe you're not a trumpet player, but there are many other ways to "rally the troops" in your life. Today, brainstorm five to six creative ways to encourage and support the people who are helping your rebuilding efforts. Then choose how often—whether it is every week or every month—you will put one of these steps into action.

I plan to rally the troops every _____
until this project or process is finished.

For Next Week: Use the space below to write any key insights or questions from your personal study that you want to discuss at the next group meeting. In preparation for next week, review chapters 19–22 in *The Nehemiah Code.*

NEVER CUT WHAT CAN BE UNTIED

Nehemiah 5:1–13

Rebuilders patiently work through the knots of interpersonal relationships instead of just cutting them off and going on about life. They recognize that relationships, like shoelaces, can be tied again if they are not severed. If we have any hope of rebuilding, we must leave our pocketknives in our pockets and avoid the temptation to whip them out and lop off the gnarled knots of twisted relationships. Successful rebuilders know this. When tensions build up, it takes patience and perseverance, determination and dedication to untie tense situations.

O.S. HAWKINS

WELCOME

King Solomon wrote, "To everything there is a season, a time for every purpose under heaven" (Ecclesiastes 3:1). This is true when it comes to our rebuilding efforts. There are times when we need to *stand up* for what we believe. There are times when we need to *back off* and figure out our next move. And there are times we need to *give in* when it's not important.

In 1977, engineer William LeMessurier was faced with an interesting challenge. He had been hired to design a new headquarters for Citibank in New York City, but the church that occupied the lot had put restrictions on where he could build. The proposed skyscraper could not encroach on the church grounds, but it could be built in the airspace above.[1] So LeMessurier came up with the idea of building the skyscraper on stilts. This feature, along with the 45-degree angled top, made it one of the most distinctive buildings in New York's skyline.

But, as it turns out, not the safest. In June 1978, a Princeton engineering student named Diane Hartley saw the building and questioned whether it could withstand high winds. Although she could have been intimidated in challenging a designer of LeMessurier's stature, she decided to take a stand and make a phone call. The company assured her the framework could withstand the strongest winds. But Hartley's call prompted them to recheck the math . . . and when they did, they were horrified to find she was right. In the end, repairs were made to strengthen the structure. Hartley's call saved hundreds—if not *thousands*—of lives.[2]

You may never know how your actions will impact others. But as we will see today, great things can happen when you take a stand . . . and handle conflict in the right way.

SHARE

Begin your group time by inviting anyone to share his or her insights from last week's personal study. Next, to kick things off, discuss one of the following questions:

- When was a time that you felt the need to *take a stand* and hold your ground? What about the situation compelled you to follow that course?

—or—

- When is a time that you felt the need to *back off* on a position that you held? What happened as a result of your willingness to seek compromise?

READ

Invite someone to read aloud the following passage. Listen for fresh insight and share any new thoughts with the group through the questions that follow.

And there was a great outcry of the people and their wives against their Jewish brethren. For there were those who said,

"We, our sons, and our daughters are many; therefore let us get grain, that we may eat and live."

There were also some who said, "We have mortgaged our lands and vineyards and houses, that we might buy grain because of the famine."

There were also those who said, "We have borrowed money for the king's tax on our lands and vineyards. Yet now our flesh is as the flesh of our brethren, our children as their children; and indeed we are forcing our sons and our daughters to be slaves, and some of our daughters have been brought into slavery. It is not in our power to redeem them, for other men have our lands and vineyards."

And I became very angry when I heard their outcry and these words. After serious thought, I rebuked the nobles and rulers, and said to them, "Each of you is exacting usury from his brother." So I called a great assembly against them. And I said to them, "According to our ability we have redeemed our Jewish brethren who were sold to the nations. Now indeed, will you even sell your brethren? Or should they be sold to us?"

Then they were silenced and found nothing to say. Then I said, "What you are doing is not good. Should you not walk in the fear of our God because of the reproach of the nations, our enemies? I also, with my brethren and my servants, am lending them money and grain. Please, let us stop this usury! Restore now to them, even this day, their lands, their vineyards, their olive groves, and their houses, also a hundredth of the money and the grain, the new wine and the oil, that you have charged them."

So they said, "We will restore it, and will require nothing from them; we will do as you say."

Then I called the priests, and required an oath from them that they would do according to this promise. Then I shook out the fold of my garment and said, "So may God shake out each man from his house, and from his property, who does not perform this promise. Even thus may he be shaken out and emptied."

And all the assembly said, "Amen!" and praised the Lord. Then the people did according to this promise (Nehemiah 5:1–13).

◆ What is one key insight that stands out to you from this passage?

◆ What was the situation that compelled Nehemiah to take action?

WATCH

Play the video for session five. As you and your group watch, use the following outline to record any thoughts or key points that stand out to you.

Notes

Knots come in relationships, and instead of taking the time to untie them (so they can be tied again), many choose to just cut them off.

Step 1 in untying knotted relationships is to *know there is a time to back off*. Nehemiah demonstrated this by . . .

Step 2 in untying knotted relationships is to *know there is a time to stand up*. Nehemiah demonstrated this by . . .

Step 3 in untying knotted relationships is to *know there is a time to give in*. Nehemiah demonstrated this by . . .

Step 4 in untying knotted relationships is to *know there is a time to reach out.* Nehemiah demonstrated this by . . .

Jesus followed this pattern of Nehemiah:

- He backed off when he . . .

- He stood up to . . .

- He gave in when he . . .

DISCUSS

Take a few minutes with your group members to discuss what you just watched and explore these concepts together.

1   When is a time in your life when you chose to "untie" a knotted relationship issue instead of cutting ties with the person? What happened as result?

2   How do you typically handle conflicts in your life? Do you tend to jump into it at the first provocation or try to avoid it at all costs? Explain.

3   How did Nehemiah respond when he heard that the wealthier inhabitants of Jerusalem were taking advantage of their less-fortunate countrymen? What can you learn from his example of taking a moment to back off (and cool off) before taking action?

4 How did Nehemiah stand up for what he believed in this situation? What do you learn from his example about how to handle conflicts appropriately?

5 What are some of the ways Nehemiah gave in when dealing with parties he was confronting? What struggles do you have in this area of "giving in" during an argument?

6 How did Nehemiah reach out to the parties he was confronting and get their agreement at a resolution? When are some times you have done this in your life?

RESPOND

Briefly review the outline for the video teaching and any notes you took. In the space below, write down the most significant point you took away from this session.

PRAY

End the gathering by partnering with one or two people from your group and praying for one another. Pray especially that God would help you to put into practice the principles you learned this week about resolving conflicts in your lives. Write down any specific requests in the space below so you can remember to continue praying throughout the week.

BETWEEN-SESSIONS PERSONAL STUDY

*R*ebuilders recognize that conflicts happen in every relationship . . . but that this doesn't mean the relationship has to come to an end because of it. This week, spend some time with God each day to see what the Bible says about knowing when to back off, when to stand up, when to give in, and when to reach out. Be sure to read the reflection questions after each activity and make a few notes in your guide about the experience. At the start of the next session, you will have a few minutes to share any insights you learned.

KNOW WHEN TO BACK OFF

As previously noted, the conflict that Nehemiah faced did not always come from outside enemies. Sometimes, as we see in chapter five, the conflict came from within. In this case, the wealthier Jews were taking advantage of their poorer neighbors during a time of famine. As might be expected, Nehemiah became angry when he heard the news. And while there are typically two common reactions to anger—either blow up or stuff it down inside—Nehemiah chose to step back and cool down. In other words, he knew *when to back off.* Consider your own typical responses to anger as you reflect on the following questions.

1 How do you tend to respond when you're angry? Do you blow up, repress it, or take time to step back and listen to your heart?

2 What kind of response to anger was modeled for you as you were growing up?

3 How do you feel, or what do you think about, the way you respond when you're angry?

4 If you could change one thing about the way you respond when you're angry, what would it be?

5 What stands out to you about the way Nehemiah responded to his anger?

6 How would things change for you if you adopted this response? How would things change if you took some time to step back and listen to your heart?

7 What keeps you from changing the way you respond when you're angry?

8 What specific action steps will you take to change your response and back off next time you're angry?

Read Numbers 14:1–19. In this passage, God was angry toward the Israelites for their rebellious attitudes. But at one point, Moses reminds God (and the Israelites) that "the LORD is longsuffering and abundant in mercy, forgiving iniquity and transgression" (verse 18). Today, ask God to help you have this same response when you are angry. Thank Him for the compassionate forgiveness He has given to you and ask for the courage to extend the same love and forgiveness to those whom have wronged you.

KNOW WHEN TO STAND UP

Unlike many people today, Nehemiah had the courage to confront. He knew when to *back off,* but he also knew when to *stand up* in order to resolve the conflict. His example reminds us that conflict resolution doesn't mean giving in at all costs. Knowing when to stand up requires us to be peacemakers, not just peacekeepers. And it requires us to have a healthy perspective of what it means to "fear the Lord"—to not want to lose God's favor and miss out on the blessings that He has for us. Consider these ideas as you respond to the following questions.

1. What do you notice about the way Nehemiah handles conflict by knowing when to stand up?

2. How does Nehemiah's story encourage or inspire you to know when to stand up?

3. How was conflict resolution modeled for you in your family, school, or job experiences?

4 When was a time you experienced *healthy* conflict
   resolution? When was a time you experienced *unhealthy*
   conflict resolution?

5 Is there an area of conflict in your life that needs resolved
   right now? If so, how can you stand up for what's right?

6 What does it mean for you to "fear the Lord"? How does
   your response to God influence your response to conflict
   resolution?

7 Who in your life needs you to stand up for them right now?

8 What are a few ways you could resolve conflict or make peace by standing up for people and principles in the midst of your rebuilding process?

Read James 1:19-27. In these verses, James provides a few "ground rules" about anger and ways to live out our faith. Some of these ways involve knowing when to stand up for the "orphans and widows in their trouble" (verse 27). Today, pray that God would give you the courage to *stand up* for someone or something as you work to resolve conflict in your everyday life. Thank Him for His calming presence as you step into situations that are not always comfortable to you.

KNOW WHEN TO GIVE IN

When it came to conflict, Nehemiah knew when to back off, when to stand up, and when to *give in*. At one point, he admits, "I also, with my brethren and my servants, am lending them money and grain. Please, let us stop this usury!" (Nehemiah 5:10). He asks everyone, himself included, to stop lending money with such high interest rates.

It is important to note that Nehemiah did not respond to the people with accusations. He did just the opposite by *giving in* with a soft response to admit his own guilt in the matter—and then he called the people to change the course of their actions. This wasn't a sign of weakness for Nehemiah to respond this way . . . it was actually a sign of great strength.

1 What stands out to you about Nehemiah's response and his actions in this situation?

2 What thoughts, feelings, or emotions do you think Nehemiah was experiencing?

3 How do you think the people whom Nehemiah was confronting felt toward him? How do you think they responded to him in the moment?

4 Have you ever had to admit your own wrongdoing in front of your peers, your team, or your loved ones? If so, what was the situation? What was the outcome?

5 What was that like for you to admit your own wrongdoing? How did you feel as a result of your confession?

6 Have you ever had a past boss, leader, parent, or coach admit his or her own wrongdoing to you? What was that like for you?

7 In what ways do you think Nehemiah's confession strengthened his relationship with the people who were rebuilding the wall?

8 In what ways have your relationships been strengthened by your willingness to give in on your own account or on the account of one of your leaders or mentors?

Read Philemon 1:1–25. This letter, written by the apostle Paul, is a case study in the art of conflict resolution. At the end of the letter, Paul asks his friend Philemon to prepare a guest room for him to stay overnight once their friendship is restored. What a beautiful picture of healthy conflict resolution! Today, ask God to show where you need to confess or give in and acknowledge your wrongdoings. Thank Him for the love and forgiveness with which He responds to your wrongdoings, and ask Him to give you the courage to face the consequences of your decisions as you give in and seek to make things right again.

KNOW WHEN TO REACH OUT

Nehemiah also knew that when it comes to conflict, it is important to *know when to reach out* in order to rebuild a community and a consensus. Nehemiah reached out to re-engage the Jews so they would finish the wall with him. Just as he did when he "rallied the troops," he got them to move past the immediate obstacle and focus on the larger goal of finishing the wall.

As believers in Christ, we have all been called to the higher mission of sharing the gospel to the world and building up the body of Christ. For this reason, it is critical to reach out to those with whom you have conflicts and re-engage with them. With this in mind, think about whether there are any relationships that you need to repair, and then engage that person in conversation. If you're not sure where to start, you could begin by saying, "Help me understand why you're so frustrated or why you're ready to quit."

Once you have done this . . . actually *listen* to the answer. Don't try to fix or solve the problem until the person has said everything that he or she needs to say. And then ask for that person's help in resolving the issue so you can move forward.

For Next Week: Use the space below to write any key insights or questions from your personal study that you want to discuss at the next group meeting. In preparation for next week, review chapters 23–24 and the Epilogue in *The Nehemiah Code.*

FINISH STRONG

Nehemiah 6:1–16

At last, the goal was in sight. "Mission Accomplished" just ahead. But be warned: this is the most dangerous point in any rebuilding process. This is when the enemy comes with one final attempt to divert us from our goal. . . . Of all the things one could say about Nehemiah, the best is that he finished strong. And before he steps off the scene of Scripture, he leaves us with a valuable lesson on how we can do the same. It is not so much how long our personal race may be, nor how difficult the obstacles we face along the way, but how we finish that matters most.

O.S. HAWKINS

WELCOME

At the beginning of this study, we looked at the story of the Espada Mission, which was built by Spanish missionaries in 1690. Although the priests set out to get started right by building a mission that would last and created relationships with the local Hasinai people, life in the hostile environment proved to be difficult. In its first two years of existence, the mission endured a flood, then a drought, and then a small-pox epidemic that killed half the local population.[1] Fearing a revolt, the priests buried the mission bell and retreated to Mexico.[2]

Fortunately, the story of the Espada Mission does not end there. In 1716, the priests returned and rebuilt the mission. This time, a conflict between France and Spain forced them to abandon it three years later. Again they persevered—determining to finish strong—and returned to rebuild in 1721. But a new problem emerged: the local people had lost interest in participating in mission life. So, in 1731, the mission was moved to the site where it stands today, along the San Antonio River, and given its current name.[3]

This mission soon flourished. At its height, it included a stone granary, living quarters, kilns for firing bricks and lime, and an aqueduct. The mission's ranch, located twenty-three miles to the south, had as many as 1,200 head of cattle and 4,000 sheep.[4] The perseverance of the early missionaries benefited many in the region, and today the walls and structures they built are visited by thousands of people each year as part of the National Park system.[5]

In our rebuilding efforts, we will face many obstacles and setbacks along the way. We will be tempted to give up our mission or give in to distractions along the way. This is why, as the conclusion of Nehemiah's story will reveal, it is so important for us to *finish strong*.

SHARE

Begin this final time together as a group by inviting anyone to share his or her insights from last week's personal study. Then, to kick things off, discuss one of the following questions:

- When is a time that you got lost while trying to reach a destination? What did you do to get yourself back on track?

—or—

- What are some doubts or distractions you have faced when trying to reach a goal? What did you do to get past them?

READ

Invite someone to read aloud the following passage. Listen for fresh insight and share any new thoughts with the group through the questions that follow.

Now it happened when Sanballat, Tobiah, Geshem the Arab, and the rest of our enemies heard that I had rebuilt the wall, and that there were no breaks left in it (though at that time I had not hung the doors in the gates), that Sanballat and Geshem sent to me, saying, "Come, let us meet together among the villages in the plain of Ono." But they thought to do me harm.

So I sent messengers to them, saying, "I am doing a great work, so that I cannot come down. Why should the work cease while I leave it and go down to you?"

But they sent me this message four times, and I answered them in the same manner.

Then Sanballat sent his servant to me as before, the fifth time, with an open letter in his hand. In it was written:

It is reported among the nations, and Geshem says, that you and the Jews plan to rebel; therefore, according to these rumors, you are rebuilding the wall, that you may be their king. And you have also appointed prophets to proclaim concerning you at Jerusalem, saying, "There is a king in Judah!" Now these matters will be reported to the king. So come, therefore, and let us consult together.

Then I sent to him, saying, "No such things as you say are being done, but you invent them in your own heart."

For they all were trying to make us afraid, saying, "Their hands will be weakened in the work, and it will not be done."

Now therefore, O God, strengthen my hands.

Afterward I came to the house of Shemaiah the son of Delaiah, the son of Mehetabel, who was a secret informer; and he said, "Let us meet together in the house of God, within the temple, and let us close the doors of the temple, for they are coming to kill you; indeed, at night they will come to kill you."

And I said, "Should such a man as I flee? And who is there such as I who would go into the temple to save his life? I will not go in!" Then I perceived that God had not sent him at all, but that he pronounced this prophecy against me because Tobiah and Sanballat had hired him. For this reason he was hired, that I should be afraid and act that way and sin, so that they might have cause for an evil report, that they might reproach me.

My God, remember Tobiah and Sanballat, according to these their works, and the prophetess Noadiah and the rest of the prophets who would have made me afraid.

So the wall was finished on the twenty-fifth day of Elul, in fifty-two days. And it happened, when all our enemies heard of it, and all the nations around us saw these things, that they were very disheartened in their own eyes; for they perceived that this work was done by our God (Nehemiah 6:1–16).

◆ What is one key insight that stands out to you from this passage?

◆ What are some ways that Nehemiah's enemies tried to distract him from his task?

WATCH

Play the video for session six. As you and your group watch, use the following outline to record any thoughts or key points that stand out to you.

Notes

The last lap is always the most important one in the journey.

Step 1 in finishing strong is to *stay off the side streets.* Nehemiah's enemies tried to get him on a side street by . . .

Nehemiah responded to their tactics by . . .

Step 2 in finishing strong is to *stay off the sidelines.* When Nehemiah's enemies were unable to lure him to the plains of Ono, they tried to . . .

Nehemiah responded to their tactics by . . .

God can take all things in our lives and work them together for good when we, like Nehemiah, love Him and are focused on His purposes.

DISCUSS

Take a few minutes with your group members to discuss what you just watched and explore these concepts together.

1 As you look back on Nehemiah's story, what are some of the obstacles that he had to overcome? Why was it important for him to now finish strong?

2 Why did Nehemiah's enemies try to get him on a side street? What are some ways the enemy has tried to derail your efforts as you try to follow God's will?

3 What are some lessons you have learned from Nehemiah on how to deal with rumors and people who try to discourage you?

4 What would have happened if Nehemiah had allowed himself to be distracted in his mission? What does his example say about the need to be faithful?

5 How did Nehemiah's enemies react when the people finished the wall? What does that say about how people will react to you when you finish strong?

6 What are some lessons you have learned from Nehemiah during this study on how to have a new beginning? What steps will you take to make that happen, starting today?

RESPOND

Briefly review the outline for the video teaching and any notes you took. In the space below, write down the most significant point you took away from this session.

PRAY

End the gathering by partnering with one or two people from your group and praying for one another. Pray especially that God would help you to finish strong in your rebuilding efforts by staying off the side streets and remaining faithful to your goal. Write down any specific requests in the space below so you can remember to continue praying throughout the week.

FINAL PERSONAL
STUDY

*R*ebuilders get started right. They build a team spirit. They let go without letting up. They persevere through difficulties. The never cut what can be untied. But most of all, successful rebuilders always finish strong. This week, finish this study strong by spending some time with God each day. Reflect on the material you covered during your group time by engaging in any or all of the following between-sessions activities. Be sure to share with your group leader or group members in the upcoming weeks any key points or insights that stood out to you.

STAY OFF THE SIDE STREETS

Nehemiah was on the final stretch of a fifty-two day marathon rebuilding the Jerusalem wall. By this time, he was likely feeling a mix of exhaustion and elation as the project neared completion. It would have been easy for him to ease up a bit as he neared the end. It's what many of us would have done if we were in his situation.

But Nehemiah knew better. He knew if he paused his work for any reason, he would not be doing what God had called him to do. He knew he needed to *stay off the side streets* and *stay focused* on the final completion of the wall. So, Nehemiah refused his enemies' invitations to meet on the Plains of Ono . . . and even when they turned their words into letters and started circulating rumors about him, he remained focused on *finishing strong*.

1   What stands out to you about the way Nehemiah handled his enemies and their request to meet with him?

2   How are you inspired and encouraged by Nehemiah's laser-focus on finishing the wall all the way up until the end?

3   How did Nehemiah refute and rebuke the rumors that were being told about him?

4   Have you found yourself off course or out of focus because of rumors being told about you? If so, how did you respond to those rumors?

5 Looking back, how would you respond differently to those rumors today?

6 Have you ever been tempted to let up or give up on a project or race near the end? If so, why?

7 What gave you the energy and focus to finish?

8 What steps will you take to stay off the side streets and keep focused as you finish your current rebuilding project?

Read Philippians 3:13–14. Paul was laser-focused as well in his mission. His singular goal was to *press on toward his calling in Jesus.* Today, ask God to give you that same kind of focus to pursue Him and to finish strong. Thank Him for giving you the stamina to stay focused and for rescuing you when you find yourself wandering down some unknown side street.

STAY OFF THE SIDELINES

When Nehemiah's enemies couldn't get him out to the Plains of Ono, they pulled another scheme to sideline him by asking him to meet them inside the temple in Jerusalem. They were trying to entice Nehemiah to enter the inner chambers of the temple, which only the priests were permitted to do. Nehemiah knew better than to say yes to this request.

If the Plain of Ono was a side street, going "within the temple" would have resulted in Nehemiah being taken out of the game and placed on the sidelines because of his unfaithfulness. Sadly, this happens to many people today, who get started right but then get *sidelined* when they do not choose to finish well. Whether you are rebuilding a home, a relationship, a marriage, a vocation, a business, a church, or anything else, remember that those who get the job done have at least one characteristic in common: *they finish strong.*

1 What stands out to you about this part of Nehemiah's story?

2 Knowing what you know about Nehemiah, how might this request to meet in the temple have been a temptation for Nehemiah?

3 Read 2 Chronicles 26:16–21. What happened to King Uzziah of Judah when he went into the place in the temple where only the priests were allowed to enter?

4 Consider Nehemiah's story up until this point—the point where he is almost finished with the wall. What are some other thoughts, actions, or temptations that could have put Nehemiah on the sidelines and kept him from finishing?

5 Has there been an example of a leader in your life who was sidelined for being unfaithful to finish strong? If so, what was the experience like for that leader? How did that person's life change as a result of his or her choices?

6 How about you? Has there ever been a situation or circumstance in your life when you lost focus on what was important or found yourself on the sidelines because you were unfaithful in some way? If so, how did you recover from that experience?

7 What lessons did you learn during that season of life?

8 How does Nehemiah's commitment to finish strong influence and encourage you in your own rebuilding journey?

Read 1 Kings 3:9. Make this verse your prayer today. Ask God to give you a discerning heart to govern your rebuilding process and to distinguish between right and wrong. Thank Him for the grace He so freely gives you when you make a mistake and get *sidelined* from time to time. And remember, it's never too late to ask Him for a second chance.

FINISH STRONG

It's a well-known fact that *people take note of those who finish strong.* This was certainly true of a man named John Stephen Akhwari, a marathon runner from Tanzania who competed in the 1968 Olympics. Almost halfway through the marathon, the runners were jostling for position when Akhwari fell and wounded his knee and shoulder. The Olympic medical staff, fearing he had dislocated his knee, urged him to withdraw from the race.

But Akhwari continued running, at times limping, until he crossed the finish line—almost an hour *after* most of the other competitors. At that point, the sun was setting and most of the crowd had left the stadium. Still, Akhwari was determined to cross the finish line. When asked why he pushed through his painful injuries to finish the race, he said, "My country did not send me 9,000 miles just to start the race; they sent me 9,000 miles to finish the race."[6]

Nehemiah could have said the same thing. "The King did not release me from his service and send me to *start* the wall. He sent me to *finish* the wall."

1   What did it take for Nehemiah to finish strong in those final days?

2   What will it take for you to finish strong with your rebuilding project?

3   How will you stay focused and remain faithful?

4   What actions or attitudes shown by Nehemiah will you adopt as your own?

5 How will you encourage the people around you to finish strong as well?

6 What does it look like for you to finish strong? Write your story of finishing strong in three to five brief sentences.

7 How do you feel when you read back over your brief story of finishing strong?

8 What do you want people to say about you, or your team, or your family, or your coworkers when you have finished rebuilding?

Read Romans 8:18–30. In this passage, the apostle Paul doesn't just say that *some* things work together for good, or *most* things work together for good, or even *many* things work together for good. No, he says *all* things work together for good. God can take *all* things in our lives and work them together for good when we, like Nehemiah, respond by loving God and staying focused on His purposes. Today, ask God to show you what it looks like to *finish strong*. Thank Him for working *all* things together for good in your life—even when on the surface the circumstances of your life don't seem to make sense.

IT'S NEVER TOO LATE FOR A NEW BEGINNING

By now you are well on your way with your own rebuilding project and have a vision of what it looks like to finish strong. Perhaps the reflection in this session was the very incentive you needed to finish the last few pieces of your own "wall." But the truth is that *you will never be truly finished with the process of rebuilding in your life.* You finish one rebuilding project and there's another problem to solve, relationship to mend, crisis to heal, or dream to pursue.

Maybe the *Nehemiah Code* study stirred up a few more areas that you now recognize need rebuilding in your life. If so, don't lose heart. Remember *it's never too late for a new beginning!* And you now have Nehemiah's "code" for rebuilding every time you're faced with an opportunity. So, as you close this study, write down any other rebuilding ideas that were stirred within you. Then prioritize them in order of importance, so that when the time is right, you can come back and apply the principles of the *Nehemiah Code* to finish strong.

EPILOGUE

We are all different in many ways. But we have one thing in common: *not one of us is perfect.* We are all in need of rebuilding from within. When it comes to a personal knowledge and faith in Jesus, all of us need to get started right on this journey. So let's begin as Nehemiah did.

Make an honest evaluation of your situation. The Bible says we "all have sinned and fall short of the glory of God" (Romans 3:23). We humans had a really good start. Life began wonderfully for us in Eden's garden. But when Satan cast a seed of doubt into our hearts, we fell into sin (Genesis 3), and we have been on a journey of trying to get back into God's presence ever since. You begin your inner rebuilding process when you make an honest evaluation of yourself, confessing that you have missed the mark and gone your own way.

Identify the need. There is a God-shaped vacuum in every human heart—a void that only He can fill. Fortunately, we have a Savior, Jesus, who clothed Himself in human flesh and walked among us to identify with our need. He took our sin upon Himself, dying our death so we could live His life, taking our sin so we could take His righteousness. The something you have been searching for all your life is really *Someone,* whose sweet name is Jesus.

Take personal responsibility. Our sin is so serious it necessitated the cross. We must take personal responsibility for it and acknowledge the gospel—the good news that Jesus died in our place to make a way out of what was inescapable for us. He was buried and rose again on the third day, defeating both sin and death. Taking personal responsibility means admitting that you are a sinner and putting your faith in Him and in Him alone.

Move out of your comfort zone. A personal faith means you transfer your trust in yourself over to trust in Christ alone for your salvation. Jesus is knocking on the door to your heart right now, and if you are willing to move out of your comfort zone, you can respond to Him right now. He has promised that "whoever calls on the name of the Lord shall be saved" (Romans 10:13). If this reflects the desire of your heart, pray this prayer:

Dear Lord Jesus, I know I have sinned and am undeserving of eternal life with You. Please forgive me. Thank You for taking my sin on the cross and dying in my place—dying the very death I deserve. You are the only hope of eternal salvation. I ask You right now to be the Lord and King of my life. My heart's desire is for a new beginning with You. I turn my face to You, accepting Your gracious gift of forgiveness and eternal life. Thank You, Lord, for coming into my life and becoming my personal Lord and Savior. In Jesus' name, amen.

If this prayer expresses the desire of your heart, you can claim the promise Jesus made to all who would choose to follow Him: "Most assuredly... he who believes in Me has everlasting life" (John 6:47).

Now that you have gotten started right on your own spiritual journey, you are ready for the great adventure for which Christ created you in the first place: to know your Lord in the intimacy of Father and child and to walk with Him daily from this day forward. Follow Nehemiah's example as you travel along your own journey and finish strong. Stay off the side streets. Keep focused. Stay off the sidelines. Keep faithful.

As we leave our friend Nehemiah, and the many truths he has given us, we can now testify ourselves to the beautiful reality... *it's never too late for a new beginning!*

LEADER'S GUIDE

*T*hank you for your willingness to lead your group through this study! What you have chosen to do is valuable and will make a great difference in the lives of others. The rewards of being a leader are different from those of participating, and we hope that as you lead you will find your own walk with Jesus deepened by this experience.

The Nehemiah Code is a six-session study built around video content and small-group interaction. As the group leader, just think of yourself as the host of a dinner party. Your job is to take care of your guests by managing all the behind-the-scenes details so that when everyone arrives, they can just enjoy time together.

As the group leader, your role is not to answer all the questions or reteach the content—the video, book, and study guide will do most of that work. Your job is to guide the experience and cultivate your small group into a kind of teaching community. This will make it a place for members to process, question, and reflect—not receive more instruction.

Before your first meeting, make sure everyone in the group gets a copy of the study guide. This will keep everyone on the same page and help the process run more smoothly. If some group members are unable to purchase the guide, arrange it so that people can share the resource with other group members. Giving everyone access to all the materials will position this study to be as rewarding an experience as possible. Everyone should feel free to write in his or her study guide and bring it to group every week.

SETTING UP THE GROUP

You will need to determine with your group how long you want to meet each week so you can plan your time accordingly. Generally, most groups like to meet for either ninety minutes or two hours, so you could use one of the following schedules:

SECTION	90 MINUTES	120 MINUTES
Welcome (members arrive and get settled)	10 minutes	15 minutes
Share (discuss one or more of the opening questions for the session)	10 minutes	15 minutes
Read (discuss the questions based on the Scripture reading for the week)	10 minutes	15 minutes
Watch (watch the teaching material together and take notes)	20 minutes	20 minutes
Discuss (discuss the Bible study questions you selected ahead of time)	30 minutes	40 minutes
Respond / Pray (pray together as a group and dismiss)	10 minutes	15 minutes

As the group leader, you'll want to create an environment that encourages sharing and learning. A church sanctuary or formal classroom may not be as ideal as a living room, because those locations can feel formal and less intimate. No matter what setting you choose, provide enough comfortable seating for everyone, and, if possible, arrange the seats in a semicircle so everyone can see the video easily. This will make transition between the video and group conversation more efficient and natural.

Also, try to get to the meeting site early so you can greet participants as they arrive. Simple refreshments create a welcoming atmosphere and can be a wonderful addition to a group study evening. Try to take food and pet allergies into account to make your guests as comfortable as possible. You may also want to consider offering childcare to couples with children who want to attend. Finally, be sure your media technology is working properly. Managing these details up front will make the rest of your group experience flow smoothly and provide a welcoming space in which to engage the content of *The Nehemiah Code*.

STARTING THE GROUP TIME

Once everyone has arrived, it's time to begin the group. Here are some simple tips to make your group time healthy, enjoyable, and effective.

First, begin the meeting with a short prayer and remind the group members to put their phones on silent. This is a way to make sure you can all be present with one another and with God. Next, give each person a few minutes to respond to the questions in the "Share" and "Read" sections. This won't require as much time in session one, but beginning in session two, people will need more time to share their insights from their personal studies. Usually, you won't answer the discussion questions yourself, but you should go first with the "Share" and "Read" questions, answering briefly and with a reasonable amount of transparency.

At the end of session one, invite the group members to complete the between-sessions personal studies for that week. Explain that you will be providing some time before the video teaching next week for anyone to share insights. Let them know sharing is optional, and it's no problem if they can't get to some of the between-sessions activities some weeks. It will still be beneficial for them to hear from the other participants and learn about what they discovered.

LEADING THE DISCUSSION TIME

Now that the group is engaged, it's time to watch the video and respond with some directed small-group discussion. Encourage all the group members to participate in the discussion, but make sure they know they don't have to do so. As the discussion progresses, you may want to follow up with comments such as, "Tell me more about that," or, "Why did you answer that way?" This will allow the group participants to deepen their reflections and invite meaningful sharing in a nonthreatening way.

Note that you have been given multiple questions to use in each session, and you do not have to use them all or even follow them in order. Feel free to pick and choose questions based on either the needs of your group or how the conversation is flowing. Also, don't be afraid of silence. Offering a question and allowing up to thirty seconds of silence is okay. It allows people space to think about how they want to respond and also gives them time to do so.

As group leader, you are the boundary keeper for your group. Do not let anyone (yourself included) dominate the group time. Keep an eye out for group members who might be tempted to "attack" folks they disagree with or try to "fix" those having struggles. These kinds of behaviors can derail a group's momentum, so they need to be steered in a different direction. Model active listening and encourage everyone in your group to do the same. This will make your group time a safe space and create a positive community.

The group discussion leads to a closing time of individual reflection and prayer. Encourage the participants to take a few moments to review what they've learned during the session and write down their thoughts to the "Respond" section. This will help them cement the big ideas in their minds as you close the session. Conclude by having the participants break into smaller groups of two to three people to pray for one another.

Thank you again for taking the time to lead your group. You are making a difference in the lives of others and having an impact on the kingdom of God!

ENDNOTES

Session 1: Get Started Right

1. Donald E. Chipman, *Spanish Texas 1519–1821* (Austin, TX: University of Texas Press, 1998), p. 89.
2. Ibid, p. 83.
3. David J. Weber, *The Spanish Frontier in North America*, Yale Western Americana Series (New Haven, CT: Yale University Press, 1992), p. 153.

Session 2: Build a Team Spirit

1. National Geodetic Survey, cited in "Washington Monument," Wikipedia, https://en.wikipedia.org/wiki/Washington_Monument.
2. Aaron V. Wunsch, *Historic American Buildings Survey, Washington Monument*, HABS DC-428, National Park Service, 1994.
3. "Monthly Visitors to the Washington Monument," *The New York Times*, data from the National Park Service, 2011, https://archive.nytimes.com/www.nytimes.com/interactive/2011/08/25/us/20110825-monthly-visitors-to-the-washington-monument.html.
4. Richard G. Weingardt, "Washington Monument: Nearly America's Very Own 'Leaning Tower of Pisa,'" *Civil and Structural Engineer*, 2014, https://csengineermag.com/article/washington-monument-nearly-americas-very-own-leaning-tower-of-pisa/.
5. "Washington Monument," National Park Service, https://www.nps.gov/wamo/learn/historyculture/index.htm.
6. John Hill, "R.I.'s Thomas Lincoln Casey, Man Behind the Washington Monument," *The Providence Journal*, 2018.
7. "Washington Monument," *Teaching with Historic Places*, National Park Service, 2006.

Endnotes

Session 3: Let Go Without Letting Up

1. Andrew Carnegie, *Autobiography of Andrew Carnegie*, edited by John C. Van Dyke (London: Constable & Company, 1920).
2. Rich Kahn, "7 Successful Entrepreneurs and How to Delegate Like Them," Business 2 Community, April 22, 2016, https://www.business2community .com/leadership/7-successful-entrepreneurs-delegate-like-01524098.
3. Ibid.
4. Andrew Carnegie, quoted in *The Outlook*, vol. 129, September–December 1921, p. 1921.
5. *Merriam-Webster's Dictionary*, s.v. "influence," https://www.merriam-web ster.com/dictionary/influence.
6. *Merriam-Webster's Dictionary*, s.v. "affirm," https://www.merriam-webster .com/dictionary/affirm; *Google Dictionary*, s.v. "affirmation," https://www.google .com/search?rlz=1C5CHFA_enUS780US780&q=Dictionary#dobs=affirmation.

Session 4: Persevere Through Difficulties

1. Amy Plitt, "Frank Lloyd Wright's Guggenheim Museum: The History of the Masterful New York Building," Curbed New York, June 8, 2017, https:// ny.curbed.com/2017/6/8/15758978/guggenheim-museum-new-york-frank -lloyd-wright-history.
2. "What Does It Mean to 'Rally the Troops'?" Quora, August 25, 2015, https:// www.quora.com/What-does-it-mean-to-rally-the-troops.

Session 5: Never Uncut What Can Be Untied

1. Matthew A. Postal, "Citicorp Center," New York City Landmarks Preservation Commission, December 10, 2018.
2. Larry Jimenez, "10 Famous Structures with Catastrophic Hidden Flaws," ListVerse, June 26, 2014, https://listverse.com/2014/06/26/10-famous -structures-with-catastrophic-hidden-flaws/.

Session 6: Finish Strong

1. Herbert Molloy Mason, Jr., *Missions of Texas* (Birmingham, AL: Southern Living Books, 1974), p. 35.
2. Ibid., p. 36
3. Gerald E. Poyo, *Tejano Origins in Eighteenth-Century San Antonio* (Austin, TX: University of Texas Press, 2011), p. 62.
4. "Mission Espada," San Antonio Missions World Heritage, 2018, https:// www.worldheritagesa.com/Missions/Mission-Espada.
5. "San Antonio Missions Park Statistics," National Park Service, February 24, 2015, https://www.nps.gov/saan/learn/management/statistics.htm.
6. Stan Isaacs, "Bud's Olympiads Are Worth Their Weight in Gold," *Newsday*, November 5, 1991, p. 109.